Step-by-Step, Practical Recipes Simple Suppers: Contents

Simple Pasta Dishes

Often served with a delicious sauce, pasta dishes are some of the easiest of all simple supper recipes.

Simple Main Courses

Choose from simply cooked fish, chicken and beef and delicious vegetable dishes.

Simple Desserts

The desserts below are easy to make and all mouthwateringly delicious.

FLAME TREE RECIPE BOOKS

FLAME TREE has been creating family-friendly, classic and beginner recipes for our bestselling cookbooks for over 12 years now. Our mission is to offer you a wide range of expert-tested dishes, while providing clear images of the final dish so that you can match it to your own results. We hope you enjoy this super selection of recipes – there are plenty more to try! Titles in this series include:

Cupcakes • Slow Cooker • Curries Chinese • Soups • Baking Breads Cakes • Simple Suppers • Pasta Chicken • Fish & Seafood • Chocolate

For more information please visit:
www.flametreepublishing.com

Four-cheese Tagliatelle

INGREDIENTS

Serves 4

300 ml/½ pint whipping cream
4 garlic cloves, peeled and
  lightly bruised
75 g/3 oz fontina cheese, diced
75 g/3 oz Gruyère cheese, grated
75 g/3 oz mozzarella cheese,
  preferably, diced
50 g/2 oz Parmesan cheese, grated,
  plus extra to serve
salt and freshly ground black pepper
275 g/10 oz fresh green tagliatelle
1–2 tbsp freshly snipped chives
fresh basil leaves, to garnish

1 Place the whipping cream with the garlic cloves in a medium pan and heat gently until small bubbles begin to form around the edge of the pan. Using a slotted spoon, remove and discard the garlic cloves.

2 Add all the cheeses to the pan and stir until melted. Season with a little salt and a lot of black pepper. Keep the sauce warm over a low heat, but do not allow to boil.

3 Meanwhile, bring a large pan of lightly salted water to the boil. Add the tagliatelle, return to the boil and cook for 2–3 minutes, or until 'al dente'.

4 Drain the pasta thoroughly and return to the pan. Pour the sauce over the pasta, add the chives then toss lightly until well coated. Tip into a warmed serving dish or spoon onto individual plates. Garnish with a few basil leaves and serve immediately with extra Parmesan cheese.

FOOD FACT

Tagliatelle comes from Bologna, where it is usually served with a meat sauce. Green tagliatelle is generally flavoured with spinach, but it is also available flavoured with fresh herbs, which goes particularly well with the rich cheese sauce in this recipe.

Pasta & Pork Ragù .

INGREDIENTS

Serves 4

1 tbsp sunflower oil
1 leek, trimmed and thinly sliced
225 g/8 oz pork fillet, diced
1 garlic clove, peeled and crushed
2 tsp paprika
¼ tsp cayenne pepper
150 ml/¼ pint white wine
600 ml/1 pint vegetable stock
400g can borlotti beans, drained
  and rinsed
2 carrots, peeled and diced
salt and freshly ground black pepper
225 g/8 oz fresh egg tagliatelle
1 tbsp freshly chopped parsley,
  to garnish
crème fraîche, to serve

FOOD FACT

Pork fillet, also commonly known as tenderloin, is a very lean and tender cut of pork. It needs little cooking time, so is perfect for this quick and simple dish. Rump or sirloin steak or boneless skinned chicken breast, cut into thin strips, could be used instead.

1 Heat the sunflower oil in a large frying pan. Add the sliced leek and cook, stirring frequently, for 5 minutes, or until softened. Add the pork and cook, stirring, for 4 minutes, or until sealed.

2 Add the crushed garlic, paprika and cayenne pepper to the pan and stir until all the pork is lightly coated in the garlic and pepper mixture.

3 Pour in the wine and 450 ml/¾ pint of the vegetable stock. Add the borlotti beans and carrots and season to taste with salt and pepper. Bring the sauce to the boil, then lower the heat and simmer for 5 minutes.

4 Meanwhile, place the egg tagliatelle in a large saucepan of lightly salted, boiling water, cover and simmer for 5 minutes, or until the pasta is cooked 'al dente'.

5 Drain the pasta, then add to the pork ragù and toss well. Adjust the seasoning, then tip into a warmed serving dish. Sprinkle with chopped parsley and serve with a little crème fraîche.

Pasta with Beef, Capers & Olives

INGREDIENTS

Serves 4

2 tbsp olive oil

300 g/11 oz rump steak, trimmed and
  cut into strips

4 spring onions, trimmed and sliced

2 garlic cloves, peeled and chopped

2 courgettes, trimmed and
  cut into strips

1 red pepper, deseeded and
  cut into strips

2 tsp freshly chopped oregano

2 tbsp capers, drained and rinsed

4 tbsp pitted black olives, sliced

400 g can chopped tomatoes

salt and freshly ground black pepper

450 g/1 lb fettuccine

1 tbsp freshly chopped parsley,
  to garnish

TASTY TIP

Make sure that the oil in the pan is hot so that the strips of beef sizzle when added. Pat the beef dry with absorbent kitchen paper and cook it in two batches. Tip the first batch on to a plate and reserve while cooking the second, then return to the pan with any juices.

1 Heat the olive oil in a large frying pan over a high heat. Add the steak and cook, stirring, for 3–4 minutes, or until browned. Remove from the pan using a slotted spoon and reserve.

2 Lower the heat, add the spring onions and garlic to the pan and cook for 1 minute. Add the courgettes and pepper and cook for 3–4 minutes.

3 Add the oregano, capers and olives to the pan with the chopped tomatoes. Season to taste with salt and pepper, then simmer for 7 minutes, stirring occasionally. Return the beef to the pan and simmer for 3–5 minutes, or until the sauce has thickened slightly.

4 Meanwhile, bring a large pan of lightly salted water to a rolling boil. Add the pasta and cook according to the packet instructions, or until 'al dente'.

5 Drain the pasta thoroughly. Return to the pan and add the beef sauce. Toss gently until the pasta is lightly coated. Tip into a warmed serving dish or onto individual plates. Sprinkle with chopped parsley and serve immediately.

Spaghetti Bolognese

INGREDIENTS

Serves 4

1 carrot
2 celery stalks
1 onion
2 garlic cloves
450 g/1 lb lean minced beef steak
225 g/8 oz smoked streaky
  bacon, chopped
1 tbsp plain flour
150 ml/¼ pint red wine
379 g can chopped tomatoes
2 tbsp tomato purée
2 tsp dried mixed herbs
salt and freshly ground black pepper
pinch of sugar
350 g/12 oz spaghetti
sprigs of fresh oregano, to garnish
shavings of Parmesan cheese,
  to serve

TASTY TIP

To make lasagne instead, layer up the sauce with sheets of fresh or precooked lasagne and top with a ready-made bechamel sauce and Parmesan cheese. Bake for 30–40 minutes in a preheated oven 190°C/375°F/Gas Mark 5, or until bubbling and the top is golden.

1 Peel and chop the carrot, trim and chop the celery, then peel and chop the onion and garlic. Heat a large, non-stick frying pan and sauté the beef and bacon for 5–10 minutes, stirring occasionally, until browned. Add the prepared vegetables to the frying pan and cook for about 3 minutes, or until softened, stirring occasionally.

2 Add the flour and cook for 1 minute. Stir in the red wine, tomatoes, tomato purée, mixed herbs, seasoning to taste and sugar. Bring to the boil, then cover and simmer for 45 minutes, stirring occasionally.

3 Meanwhile, bring a large saucepan of lightly salted water to the boil and cook the spaghetti for 10–12 minutes, or until 'al dente'. Drain well and divide between 4 serving plates. Spoon over the sauce, garnish with a few sprigs of oregano and serve immediately with plenty of Parmesan shavings.

Lamb Arrabbiata

INGREDIENTS

Serves 4

4 tbsp olive oil

450 g/1 lb lamb fillets, cubed

1 large onion, peeled and sliced

4 garlic cloves, peeled and
   finely chopped

1 red chilli, deseeded and
   finely chopped

400 g can chopped tomatoes

175 g/6 oz pitted black olives, halved

150 ml/¼ pint white wine

salt and freshly ground black pepper

275 g/10 oz farfalle pasta

1 tsp butter

4 tbsp freshly chopped parsley,
   plus 1 tbsp to garnish

HELPFUL HINT

When you are cooking pasta, remember to use a large saucepan so that the pasta has plenty of time to move around freely. Once the water has come to the boil, add the pasta, stir, cover with a lid and return to the boil. The lid can then be removed so that the water does not boil over.

1 Heat 2 tablespoons of the olive oil in a large frying pan and cook the lamb for 5–7 minutes, or until sealed. Remove from the pan using a slotted spoon and reserve.

2 Heat the remaining oil in the pan, add the onion, garlic and chilli and cook until softened. Add the tomatoes, bring to the boil, then simmer for 10 minutes.

3 Return the browned lamb to the pan with the olives and pour in the wine. Bring the sauce back to the boil, reduce the heat then simmer, uncovered, for 15 minutes, until the lamb is tender. Season to taste with salt and pepper.

4 Meanwhile, bring a large pan of lightly salted water to a rolling boil. Add the pasta and cook according to the packet instructions, or until 'al dente'.

5 Drain the pasta, toss in the butter, then add to the sauce and mix lightly. Stir in 4 tablespoons of the chopped parsley, then tip into a warmed serving dish. Sprinkle with the remaining parsley and serve immediately.

Gingered Cod Steaks

INGREDIENTS

Serves 4

2.5 cm/1 inch piece fresh root
  ginger, peeled
4 spring onions
2 tsp freshly chopped parsley
1 tbsp soft brown sugar
4 x 175 g/6 oz thick cod steaks
salt and freshly ground black pepper
25 g/1 oz half-fat butter
freshly cooked vegetables, to serve

TASTY TIP

Why not try serving this dish with some roasted new potatoes baked in paper. Place the new potatoes into double thickness greaseproof paper with a few cloves of peeled garlic. Drizzle with a little olive oil and season well with salt and black pepper. Fold all the edges of the greaseproof paper together and roast in the oven at 180°C/350°F/Gas Mark 4 for 40–50 minutes before serving in the paper casing.

1 Preheat the grill and line the grill rack with a layer of tinfoil. Coarsely grate the piece of ginger. Trim the spring onions and cut into thin strips.

2 Mix the spring onions, ginger, chopped parsley and sugar. Add 1 tablespoon of water.

3 Wipe the fish steaks. Season to taste with salt and pepper. Place onto 4 separate 20.5 x 20.5 cm/8 x 8 inch tinfoil squares.

4 Carefully spoon the spring onions and ginger mixture over the fish.

5 Cut the butter into small cubes and place over the fish.

6 Loosely fold the foil over the steaks to enclose the fish and to make a parcel.

7 Place under the preheated grill and cook for 10–12 minutes or until cooked and the flesh has turned opaque.

8 Place the fish parcels on individual serving plates. Serve immediately with the freshly cooked vegetables.

Battered Cod & Chunky Chips

INGREDIENTS

Serves 4

15 g/½ oz fresh yeast
300 ml/½ pint beer
225 g/8 oz plain flour
1 tsp salt
700 g/1½ lb potatoes
450 ml/¾ pint groundnut oil
4 cod fillets, about 225 g/8 oz each,
    skinned and boned
2 tbsp seasoned plain flour

To garnish:
lemon wedges
sprigs of flat-leaf parsley

To serve:
tomato ketchup
vinegar

FOOD FACT
Fresh yeast can be bought in health food shops, large supermarkets with in-store bakeries and some bakers. Check that it is moist and creamy-coloured and has a strong yeasty smell. If it is dry, discoloured and crumbly, it is probably stale and will not work very well.

1 Dissolve the yeast with a little of the beer in a jug and mix to a paste. Pour in the remaining beer, whisking all the time until smooth. Place the flour and salt in a bowl, and gradually pour in the beer mixture, whisking continuously to make a thick smooth batter. Cover the bowl and allow the batter to stand at room temperature for 1 hour.

2 Peel the potatoes and cut into thick slices. Cut each slice lengthways to make chunky chips. Place them in a non-stick frying pan and heat, shaking the pan until all the moisture has evaporated. Turn them out on absorbent kitchen paper to dry off.

3 Heat the oil to 180°C/350°F, then fry the chips a few at a time for 4–5 minutes until crisp and golden. Drain on absorbent kitchen paper and keep warm.

4 Pat the cod fillets dry, then coat in the flour. Dip the floured fillets into the reserved batter. Fry for 2–3 minutes until cooked and crisp, then drain. Garnish with lemon wedges and parsley and serve immediately with the chips, tomato ketchup and vinegar.

Stir-fried Salmon with Peas

INGREDIENTS

Serves 4

450 g/1 lb salmon fillet
salt
6 slices streaky bacon
1 tbsp vegetable oil
50 ml/2 fl oz chicken or fish stock
2 tbsp dark soy sauce
2 tbsp Chinese rice wine or dry sherry
1 tsp sugar
75 g/3 oz frozen peas, thawed
1–2 tbsp freshly shredded mint
1 tsp cornflour
sprigs of fresh mint, to garnish
freshly cooked noodles, to serve

HELPFUL HINT

Sprinkling salmon with salt helps draw out some of the juices and makes the flesh firmer, so that it remains whole when cooked. Prior to cooking, pat the strips with absorbent kitchen paper to remove as much of the salty liquid as possible. Dark soy sauce is used in this recipe as it is slightly less salty than the light version.

1 Wipe and skin the salmon fillet and remove any pin bones. Slice into 2.5 cm/1 inch strips, place on a plate and sprinkle with salt. Leave for 20 minutes, then pat dry with absorbent kitchen paper and reserve.

2 Remove any cartilage from the bacon, cut into small cubes and reserve.

3 Heat a wok or large frying pan over a high heat, then add the oil and when hot, add the bacon and stir-fry for 3 minutes or until crisp and golden. Push to one side and add the strips of salmon. Stir-fry gently for 2 minutes or until the flesh is opaque.

4 Pour the chicken or fish stock, soy sauce and Chinese rice wine or sherry into the wok, then stir in the sugar, peas and freshly shredded mint.

5 Blend the cornflour with 1 tablespoon of water to form a smooth paste and stir into the sauce. Bring to the boil, reduce the heat and simmer for 1 minute, or until slightly thickened and smooth. Garnish and serve immediately with noodles.

1

3

4

Supreme Baked Potatoes

INGREDIENTS

Serves 4

4 large baking potatoes

40 g/1½ oz butter

1 tbsp sunflower oil

1 carrot, peeled and chopped

2 celery stalks, trimmed and
  finely chopped

200 g can white crab meat

2 spring onions, trimmed and
  finely chopped

salt and freshly ground black pepper

50 g/2 oz Cheddar cheese, grated

tomato salad, to serve

TASTY TIP

Threading the potatoes onto metal skewers helps them to cook more evenly and quickly as heat is transferred via the metal to the centres of the potatoes during the cooking process. To give the skins a much crunchier finish, rub them with a little oil and lightly sprinkle with salt before baking.

1 Preheat the oven to 200°C/400°F/Gas Mark 6. Scrub the potatoes and prick all over with a fork, or thread 2 potatoes onto 2 long metal skewers. Place the potatoes in the preheated oven for 1–1½ hours, or until soft to the touch. Allow to cool a little, then cut in half.

2 Scoop out the cooked potato and turn into a bowl, leaving a reasonably firm potato shell. Mash the cooked potato flesh, then mix in the butter and mash until the butter has melted.

3 While the potatoes are cooking, heat the oil in a frying pan and cook the carrot and celery for 2 minutes. Cover the pan tightly and continue to cook for another 5 minutes, or until the vegetables are tender.

4 Add the cooked vegetables to the bowl of mashed potato and mix well. Fold in the crab meat and the spring onions, then season to taste with salt and pepper.

5 Pile the mixture back into the potato shells and press in firmly. Sprinkle the grated cheese over the top and return the potato halves to the oven for 12–15 minutes until hot, golden and bubbling. Serve immediately with a tomato salad.

2

4

5

Turkey & Vegetable Stir Fry

INGREDIENTS

Serves 4

350 g/12 oz mixed vegetables, such
   as baby sweetcorn, 1 small red
   pepper, pak choi, mushrooms,
   broccoli florets and baby carrots
1 red chilli
2 tbsp groundnut oil
350 g/12 oz skinless, boneless turkey
   breast, sliced into fine strips across
   the grain
2 garlic cloves, peeled and
   finely chopped
2.5 cm/1 inch piece fresh root ginger,
   peeled and finely grated
3 spring onions, trimmed and
   finely sliced
2 tbsp light soy sauce
1 tbsp Chinese rice wine or dry sherry
2 tbsp chicken stock or water
1 tsp cornflour
1 tsp sesame oil
freshly cooked noodles or rice,
   to serve

To garnish:
50 g/2 oz toasted cashew nuts
2 spring onions, finely shredded
25 g/1 oz beansprouts

1 Slice or chop the vegetables into small pieces, depending on which you use. Halve the baby sweetcorn lengthways, deseed and thinly slice the red pepper, tear or shred the pak choi, slice the mushrooms, break the broccoli into small florets and cut the carrots into matchsticks. Deseed and finely chop the chilli.

2 Heat a wok or large frying pan, add the oil and when hot, add the turkey strips and stir-fry for 1 minute or until they turn white. Add the garlic, ginger, spring onions and chilli and cook for a few seconds.

3 Add the prepared carrot, pepper, broccoli and mushrooms and stir-fry for 1 minute. Add the baby sweetcorn and pak choi and stir-fry for 1 minute.

4 Blend the soy sauce, Chinese rice wine or sherry and stock or water and pour over the vegetables. Blend the cornflour with 1 teaspoon of water and stir into the vegetables, mixing well. Bring to the boil, reduce the heat, then simmer for 1 minute. Stir in the sesame oil. Tip into a warmed serving dish, sprinkle with cashew nuts, shredded spring onions and beansprouts. Serve immediately with noodles or rice.

Sweet-&-Sour Rice with Chicken

INGREDIENTS

Serves 4

4 spring onions
2 tsp sesame oil
1 tsp Chinese five-spice powder
450 g/1 lb chicken breast,
  cut into cubes
1 tbsp oil
1 garlic clove, peeled and crushed
1 medium onion, peeled and sliced
  into thin wedges
225 g/8 oz long-grain white rice
600 ml/1 pint water
4 tbsp tomato ketchup
1 tbsp tomato purée
2 tbsp honey
1 tbsp vinegar
1 tbsp dark soy sauce
1 carrot, peeled and cut
  into matchsticks

FOOD FACT

Five-spice powder is a very popular Chinese seasoning. It can be bought ready-blended in jars and is a mixture of finely ground star anise, fennel, cinnamon, cloves and Sichuan pepper. It adds a unique aniseed flavour to food.

1 Trim the spring onions, then cut lengthways into fine strips. Drop into a large bowl of iced water and reserve.

2 Mix together the sesame oil and Chinese five-spice powder and use to rub into the cubed chicken. Heat the wok, then add the oil and, when hot, cook the garlic and onion for 2–3 minutes, or until transparent and softened.

3 Add the chicken and stir-fry over a medium-high heat until the chicken is golden and cooked through. Using a slotted spoon, remove from the wok and keep warm.

4 Stir the rice into the wok and add the water, tomato ketchup, tomato purée, honey, vinegar and soy sauce. Stir well to mix. Bring to the boil, then simmer until almost all of the liquid is absorbed. Stir in the carrot and reserved chicken and continue to cook for 3–4 minutes.

5 Drain the spring onions, which will have become curly. Garnish with the spring onion curls and serve immediately with the rice and chicken.

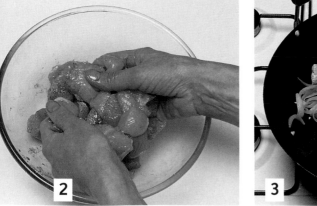

Turkey Hash with Potato & Beetroot

INGREDIENTS

Serves 4–6

2 tbsp vegetable oil

50 g/2 oz butter

4 slices streaky bacon, diced or sliced

1 medium onion, peeled and
 finely chopped

450 g/1 lb cooked turkey, diced

450 g/1 lb finely chopped
 cooked potatoes

2–3 tbsp freshly chopped parsley

2 tbsp plain flour

250 g/9 oz cooked medium
 beetroot, diced

green salad, to serve

TASTY TIP

A hash is usually made just with potatoes, but here they are combined with ruby red beetroot, which adds vibrant colour and a sweet earthy flavour to the dish. Make sure that you buy plainly cooked beetroot, rather than the type preserved in vinegar.

1 In a large, heavy based frying pan, heat the oil and half the butter over a medium heat until sizzling. Add the bacon and cook for 4 minutes, or until crisp and golden, stirring occasionally. Using a slotted spoon, transfer to a large bowl. Add the onion to the pan and cook for 3–4 minutes, or until soft and golden, stirring frequently.

2 Meanwhile, add the turkey, potatoes, parsley and flour to the cooked bacon in the bowl. Stir and toss gently, then fold in the diced beetroot.

3 Add half the remaining butter to the frying pan and then the turkey vegetable mixture. Stir, then spread the mixture to evenly cover the bottom of the frying pan. Cook for 15 minutes, or until the underside is crisp and brown, pressing the hash firmly into a cake with a spatula. Remove from the heat.

4 Invert a large plate over the frying pan and, holding the plate and frying pan together with an oven glove, turn the hash out onto the plate. Heat the remaining butter in the pan, slide the hash back into the pan and cook for 4 minutes, or until crisp and brown on the other side. Invert onto the plate again and serve immediately with a green salad.

Beef Fajitas with Avocado Sauce

INGREDIENTS

Serves 3–6

2 tbsp sunflower oil

450 g/1 lb beef fillet or rump steak,
   trimmed and cut into thin strips

2 garlic cloves, peeled and crushed

1 tsp ground cumin

¼ tsp cayenne pepper

1 tbsp paprika

230 g can chopped tomatoes

215 g can red kidney beans, drained

1 tbsp freshly chopped coriander

1 avocado, peeled, pitted
   and chopped

1 shallot, peeled and chopped

1 large tomato, skinned, deseeded
   and chopped

1 red chilli, diced

1 tbsp lemon juice

6 large flour tortilla pancakes

3–4 tbsp soured cream

green salad, to serve

HELPFUL HINT

The avocado sauce should not be made too far in advance, as it has a tendency to discolour. If it is necessary to make it some time ahead, the surface of the sauce should be covered with clingfilm.

1 Heat the wok, add the oil, then stir-fry the beef for 3–4 minutes. Add the garlic and spices and continue to cook for a further 2 minutes. Stir the tomatoes into the wok, bring to the boil, cover and simmer gently for 5 minutes.

2 Meanwhile, blend the kidney beans in a food processor until slightly broken up, then add to the wok. Continue to cook for a further 5 minutes, adding 2–3 tablespoons of water. The mixture should be thick and fairly dry. Stir in the chopped coriander.

3 Mix the chopped avocado, shallot, tomato, chilli and lemon juice together. Spoon into a serving dish and reserve.

4 When ready to serve, warm the tortillas and spread with a little soured cream. Place a spoonful of the beef mixture on top, followed by a spoonful of the avocado sauce, then roll up. Repeat until all the mixture is used up. Serve immediately with a green salad.

Fillet Steaks with Tomato & Garlic Sauce

INGREDIENTS

Serves 4

700 g/1½ lb ripe tomatoes
2 garlic cloves
2 tbsp olive oil
2 tbsp freshly chopped basil
2 tbsp freshly chopped oregano
2 tbsp red wine
salt and freshly ground black pepper
75 g/3 oz pitted black olives, chopped
4 fillet steaks, about 175 g/6 oz each
freshly cooked vegetables, to serve

1 Make a small cross on the top of each tomato and place in a large bowl. Cover with boiling water and leave for 2 minutes. Using a slotted spoon, remove the tomatoes and skin carefully. Repeat until all the tomatoes are skinned. Place on a chopping board, cut into quarters, remove the seeds and roughly chop, then reserve.

2 Peel and chop the garlic. Heat half the olive oil in a saucepan and cook the garlic for 30 seconds. Add the chopped tomatoes with the basil, oregano, red wine and season to taste with salt and pepper. Bring to the boil then reduce the heat, cover and simmer for 15 minutes, stirring occasionally, or until the sauce is reduced and thickened. Stir the olives into the sauce and keep warm while cooking the steaks.

3 Meanwhile, lightly oil a griddle pan or heavy based frying pan with the remaining olive oil and cook the steaks for 2 minutes on each side to seal. Continue to cook the steaks for a further 2–4 minutes, depending on personal preference. Serve the steaks immediately with the garlic sauce and freshly cooked vegetables.

FOOD FACT

Quality fillet steak should come with a deep mahogany colour with a good marbling of fat. If the meat is bright red, or if the fat is bright white, the meat has not been aged properly and will probably be quite tough.

Leek & Ham Risotto

INGREDIENTS

Serves 4

1 tbsp olive oil
25 g/1 oz butter
1 medium onion, peeled and
  finely chopped
4 leeks, trimmed and thinly sliced
1¹/₂ tbsp freshly chopped thyme
350 g/12 oz Arborio rice
1.4 litres/2¹/₄ pints vegetable or
  chicken stock, heated
225 g/8 oz cooked ham
175 g/6 oz peas, thawed if frozen
50 g/2 oz Parmesan cheese, grated
salt and freshly ground black pepper

HELPFUL HINT

Risotto should take only about 15 minutes to cook, so taste it after this time – the rice should be creamy with just a slight bite to it. If it is not quite ready, continue adding the stock, a little at a time, and cook for a few more minutes. Stop as soon as it tastes ready as you do not have to add all of the liquid.

1 Heat the oil and half the butter together in a large saucepan. Add the onion and leeks and cook over a medium heat for 6–8 minutes, stirring occasionally, until soft and beginning to colour. Stir in the thyme and cook briefly.

2 Add the rice and stir well. Continue stirring over a medium heat for about 1 minute until the rice is glossy. Add a ladleful or two of the stock and stir well until the stock is absorbed. Continue adding stock, a ladleful at a time, and stirring well between additions, until about two-thirds of the stock has been added.

3 Meanwhile, either chop or finely shred the ham, then add to the saucepan of rice together with the peas. Continue adding ladlefuls of stock, as described in step 2, until the rice is tender and the ham is heated through thoroughly.

4 Add the remaining butter, sprinkle over the Parmesan cheese and season to taste with salt and pepper. When the butter has melted and the cheese has softened, stir well to incorporate. Taste and adjust the seasoning, then serve immediately.

Pork Sausages with Onion Gravy & Best-ever Mash

INGREDIENTS

Serves 4

50 g/2 oz butter
1 tbsp olive oil
2 large onions, peeled and
  thinly sliced
pinch of sugar
1 tbsp freshly chopped thyme
1 tbsp plain flour
100 ml/3½ fl oz Madeira
200 ml/7 fl oz vegetable stock
8–12 good-quality butchers pork
  sausages, depending on size

For the mash:

900 g/2 lb floury potatoes, peeled
75 g/3 oz butter
4 tbsp crème fraîche or soured cream
salt and freshly ground black pepper

FOOD FACT

These days, there is a huge range of regional pork sausages to choose from. Why not try meaty Cambridge sausages packed with herbs and spices, or Cumberland sausages made from coarsely chopped pork and black pepper.

1 Melt the butter with the oil and add the onions. Cover and cook gently for about 20 minutes until the onions have collapsed. Add the sugar and stir well. Uncover and continue to cook, stirring often, until the onions are very soft and golden. Add the thyme, stir well, then add the flour, stirring. Gradually add the Madeira and the stock. Bring to the boil and simmer gently for 10 minutes.

2 Meanwhile, put the sausages in a large frying pan and cook over a medium heat for about 15–20 minutes, turning often, until golden brown and slightly sticky all over.

3 For the mash, boil the potatoes in plenty of lightly salted water for 15–18 minutes until tender. Drain well and return to the saucepan. Put the saucepan over a low heat to allow the potatoes to dry thoroughly. Remove from the heat and add the butter, crème fraîche and salt and pepper. Mash thoroughly. Serve the potato mash topped with the sausages and onion gravy.

1

2

3

Pork Goulash & Rice

INGREDIENTS

Serves 4

700 g/1½ lb boneless pork rib chops
1 tbsp olive oil
2 onions, peeled and
 roughly chopped
1 red pepper, deseeded and
 sliced thinly
1 garlic clove, peeled and crushed
1 tbsp plain flour
1 rounded tbsp paprika
400 g can chopped tomatoes
salt and freshly ground black pepper
250 g/9 oz long-grain white rice
450 ml/¾ pint chicken stock
sprigs of fresh flat-leaf parsley,
 to garnish
150 ml/¼ pint soured cream,
 to serve

FOOD FACT

Paprika is the ground red powder derived from the dried pepper *Capsicum annum* and is a vital ingredient of goulash, giving it a distinctive colour and taste.

1 Preheat the oven to 140°C/275°F/Gas Mark 1. Cut the pork into large cubes, about 4 cm/1½ inches square. Heat the oil in a large flameproof casserole dish and brown the pork in batches over a high heat, transferring the cubes to a plate as they brown.

2 Over a medium heat, add the onions and pepper and cook for about 5 minutes, stirring regularly, until they begin to brown. Add the garlic and return the meat to the casserole dish along with any juices on the plate. Sprinkle in the flour and paprika and stir well to soak up the oil and juices.

3 Add the tomatoes and season to taste with salt and pepper. Bring slowly to the boil, cover with a tight-fitting lid and cook in the preheated oven for 1½ hours.

4 Meanwhile, rinse the rice in several changes of water until the water remains relatively clear. Drain well and put into a saucepan with the chicken stock or water and a little salt. Cover tightly and bring to the boil. Turn the heat down as low as possible and cook for 10 minutes without removing the lid. After 10 minutes, remove from the heat and leave for a further 10 minutes, without removing the lid. Fluff with a fork.

5 When the meat is tender, stir in the soured cream lightly to create a marbled effect, or serve separately. Garnish with parsley and serve immediately with the rice.

Vegetable Biryani

INGREDIENTS

Serves 4

2 tbsp vegetable oil, plus a little extra
  for brushing
2 large onions, peeled and thinly
  sliced lengthways
2 garlic cloves, peeled and
  finely chopped
2.5 cm/1 inch piece fresh root ginger,
  peeled and finely grated
1 small carrot, peeled and cut
  into sticks
1 small parsnip, peeled and diced
1 small sweet potato, peeled
  and diced
1 tbsp medium curry paste
225 g/8 oz basmati rice
4 ripe tomatoes, peeled, deseeded
  and diced
600 ml/1 pint vegetable stock
175 g/6 oz cauliflower florets
50 g/2 oz peas, thawed if frozen
salt and freshly ground black pepper

To garnish:

roasted cashew nuts
raisins
fresh coriander leaves

1 Preheat the oven to 200°C/400°F/Gas Mark 6. Put 1 tablespoon of the vegetable oil in a large bowl with the onions and toss to coat. Lightly brush or spray a non-stick baking sheet with a little more oil. Spread half the onions onto the baking sheet and cook at the top of the preheated oven for 25–30 minutes, stirring regularly, until golden and crisp. Remove from the oven and reserve for the garnish.

2 Meanwhile, heat a large flameproof casserole dish over a medium heat and add the remaining oil and onions. Cook for 5–7 minutes until softened and starting to brown. Add a little water if they start to stick. Add the garlic and ginger and cook for another minute, then add the carrot, parsnip and sweet potato. Cook the vegetables for a further 5 minutes. Add the curry paste and stir for a minute until everything is coated, then stir in the rice and tomatoes. After 2 minutes add the stock and stir well. Bring to the boil, cover and simmer over a very gentle heat for about 10 minutes.

3 Add the cauliflower and peas and cook for 8–10 minutes, or until the rice is tender. Season to taste with salt and pepper. Serve garnished with the crispy onions, cashew nuts, raisins and coriander.

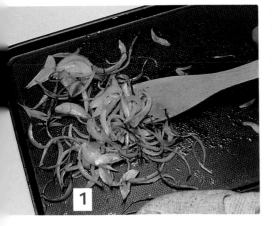

Baked Aubergines with Tomato & Mozzarella

INGREDIENTS

Serves 4

3 medium aubergines, trimmed
  and sliced
salt and freshly ground black pepper
4–6 tbsp olive oil
450 g/1 lb fresh turkey mince
1 onion, peeled and chopped
2 garlic cloves, peeled and chopped
2 x 400 g cans cherry tomatoes
1 tbsp fresh mixed herbs
200 ml/7 fl oz red wine
350 g/12 oz macaroni
5 tbsp freshly chopped basil
125 g/4 oz mozzarella cheese, drained
  and chopped
50 g/2 oz freshly grated
  Parmesan cheese

HELPFUL HINT

Aubergines are often salted to remove bitterness (although they seem to be less bitter these days). Salting also removes moisture so they absorb less oil when fried.

1 Preheat the oven to 200°C/400°F/Gas Mark 6, 15 minutes before cooking. Place the aubergine slices in a colander and sprinkle with salt. Leave for 1 hour or until the juices run clear. Rinse and dry on absorbent kitchen paper.

2 Heat 3–5 tablespoons of the olive oil in a large frying pan and cook the prepared aubergines in batches for 2 minutes on each side, or until softened. Remove and drain on absorbent kitchen paper.

3 Heat 1 tablespoon of olive oil in a saucepan, add the turkey mince and cook for 5 minutes, or until browned and sealed.

4 Add the onion to the pan and cook for 5 minutes, or until softened. Add the chopped garlic, the tomatoes and mixed herbs. Pour in the wine and season to taste with salt and pepper. Bring to the boil, lower the heat then simmer for 15 minutes, or until thickened.

5 Meanwhile, bring a large pan of lightly salted water to a rolling boil. Add the macaroni and cook according to the packet instructions, or until 'al dente'. Drain thoroughly.

6 Spoon half the tomato mixture into a lightly oiled ovenproof dish. Top with half the aubergine, pasta and chopped basil, then season lightly. Repeat the layers, finishing with a layer of aubergine. Sprinkle with the mozzarella and Parmesan cheeses, then bake in the preheated oven for 30 minutes, or until golden and bubbling. Serve immediately.

2

4

6

Chocolate Mallow Pie

INGREDIENTS

Serves 6

200 g/7 oz digestive biscuits
75 g/3 oz butter, melted
175 g/6 oz plain dark chocolate
20 marshmallows
1 medium egg, separated
300 ml/½ pint double cream

1 Place the biscuits in a polythene bag and finely crush with a rolling pin. Alternatively, place in a food processor and blend until fine crumbs are formed.

2 Melt the butter in a medium-sized saucepan, add the crushed biscuits and mix together. Press into the base of the prepared tin and leave to cool in the refrigerator.

3 Melt 125 g/4 oz of the chocolate with the marshmallows and 2 tablespoons of water in a saucepan over a gentle heat, stirring constantly. Leave to cool slightly, then stir in the egg yolk, beat well, then return to the refrigerator until cool.

4 Whisk the egg white until stiff and standing in peaks, then fold into the chocolate mixture.

5 Lightly whip the cream and fold three-quarters of the cream into the chocolate mixture. Reserve the remainder. Spoon the chocolate cream into the flan case and chill in the refrigerator until set.

6 When ready to serve, spoon the remaining cream over the chocolate pie, swirling in a decorative pattern. Grate the remaining dark chocolate and sprinkle over the cream, then serve.

TASTY TIP

Replace the digestive biscuits with the same weight of chocolate-covered digestive biscuits to make a quick change to this recipe.

Frozen Mississippi Mud Pie

INGREDIENTS

Cuts into 6–8 slices

1 quantity Ginger Crumb Crust
600 ml/1 pint chocolate ice cream
600 ml/1 pint coffee-flavoured
   ice cream

For the chocolate topping:

175 g/6 oz plain dark
   chocolate, chopped
50 ml/2 fl oz single cream
1 tbsp golden syrup
1 tsp vanilla essence
50 g/2 oz coarsely grated white and
   milk chocolate

TASTY TIP

For this delicious pie, it is a good idea to use the best-quality ice cream available. Look out for chocolate ice cream with added ingredients such as chocolate chips, pieces of toffee or rippled chocolate. If you prefer, you can add raspberries, chopped nuts or small pieces of chopped white chocolate to both chocolate and coffee ice cream.

1 Prepare the crumb crust and use to line a 23 cm/9 inch loose-based flan tin and freeze for 30 minutes.

2 Soften the ice creams at room temperature for about 25 minutes. Spoon the chocolate ice cream into the crumb crust, spreading it evenly over the base, then spoon the coffee ice cream over the chocolate ice cream, mounding it slightly in the centre. Return to the freezer to refreeze the ice cream.

3 For the topping, heat the dark chocolate with the cream, golden syrup and vanilla essence in a saucepan. Stir until the chocolate has melted and is smooth. Pour into a bowl and chill in the refrigerator, stirring occasionally, until cold but not set.

4 Spread the cooled chocolate mixture over the top of the frozen pie. Sprinkle with the chocolate and return to the freezer for 1½ hours or until firm. Serve at room temperature.

Crunchy Rhubarb Crumble

INGREDIENTS

Serves 6

125 g/4 oz plain flour
50 g/2 oz softened butter
50 g/2 oz rolled oats
50 g/2 oz demerara sugar
1 tbsp sesame seeds
½ tsp ground cinnamon
450 g/1 lb fresh rhubarb
50 g/2 oz caster sugar
custard or cream, to serve

TASTY TIP

Crumble needs custard, and to make a lovely homemade custard, pour 600 ml/1 pint of milk with a few drops of vanilla essence into a saucepan and bring to the boil. Remove from the heat and allow to cool. Meanwhile, whisk 5 egg yolks and 3 tablespoons of caster sugar together in a mixing bowl until thick and pale in colour. Add the milk, stir and strain into a heavy based saucepan. Cook the custard on a low heat, stirring constantly until the consistency of double cream. Pour over the rhubarb crumble and serve.

1 Preheat the oven to 180°C/350°F/Gas Mark 4. Place the flour in a large bowl and cut the butter into cubes. Add to the flour and rub in with the fingertips until the mixture resembles fine breadcrumbs, or blend for a few seconds in a food processor.

2 Stir in the rolled oats, demerara sugar, sesame seeds and cinnamon. Mix well and reserve.

3 Prepare the rhubarb by removing the thick ends of the stalks and cut diagonally into 2.5 cm/1 inch chunks. Wash thoroughly and pat dry with a clean tea towel. Place the rhubarb in a 1.1 litre/2 pint pie dish.

4 Sprinkle the caster sugar over the rhubarb and top with the reserved crumble mixture. Level the top of the crumble so that all the fruit is well covered and press down firmly. If liked, sprinkle the top with a little extra caster sugar.

5 Place on a baking sheet and bake in the preheated oven for 40–50 minutes, or until the fruit is soft and the topping is golden brown. Sprinkle the pudding with some more caster sugar and serve hot with custard or cream.

2

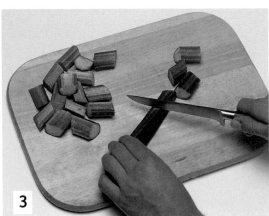
3

4

Lattice Treacle Tart

INGREDIENTS

Serves 4

For the pastry:
175 g/6 oz plain flour
40 g/1½ oz butter
40 g/1½ oz white vegetable fat

For the filling:
225 g/8 oz golden syrup
finely grated rind and juice of 1 lemon
75 g/3 oz fresh white breadcrumbs
1 small egg, beaten

1 Preheat the oven to 190°C/375°F/Gas Mark 5. Make the pastry by placing the flour, butter and white vegetable fat in a food processor. Blend in short sharp bursts until the mixture resembles fine breadcrumbs. Remove from the processor and place on a pastry board or into a large bowl.

2 Stir in enough cold water to make a dough and knead in a large bowl or on a floured surface until smooth and pliable.

3 Roll out the pastry and use to line a 20.5 cm/8 inch loose-bottomed fluted flan dish or tin. Reserve the pastry trimmings for decoration. Chill for 30 minutes.

4 Meanwhile, to make the filling, place the golden syrup in a saucepan and warm gently with the lemon rind and juice. Tip the breadcrumbs into the pastry case and pour the syrup mixture over the top.

5 Roll the pastry trimmings out onto a lightly floured surface and cut into 6–8 thin strips. Lightly dampen the pastry edge of the tart, then place the strips across the filling in a lattice pattern. Brush the ends of the strips with water and seal to the edge of the tart. Brush a little beaten egg over the pastry and bake in the preheated oven for 25 minutes, or until the filling is just set. Serve hot or cold.

TASTY TIP
To give this tart a slightly different texture and taste, why not replace the breadcrumbs with an equal amount of desiccated coconut?

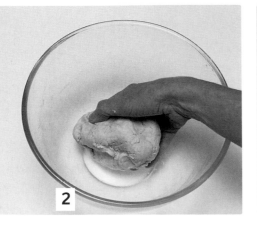

2

4

5

Step-by-Step, Practical Recipes Simple Suppers: Tips & Hints

Tasty Tip

Risotto (see p30) makes a great simple supper. For the best results, the stock to be added to the risotto should be kept at a low simmer in a separate saucepan, so that it is piping hot when added to the rice. This will ensure that the dish is kept at a constant heat during cooking, which is important if you want to achieve a perfect creamy texture.

Tasty Tip

Even if you are just cooking a quick, simple supper, if you marinade the meat or fish the night before, it can have delicious results. Marinating meat, in particular, not only adds flavour, but tenderises it as well due to the acids in the marinade liquid, which will often include lemon. Basically, the longer you marinate your food, the more the flavour will come out. As well as lemon, try other citrus juices – both orange and lime juice would be delicious.

Helpful Hint

To make your own Chinese-style vegetable stock, in order to add flavour to Chinese-style dishes (see p20 and 24), roughly chop 1 onion, 2 celery sticks and 2 carrots and place in a large saucepan with a few dried shiitake mushrooms and slices of fresh root ginger. Pour in 1.4 litres/2½ pints cold water, bring to the boil, partially cover and simmer for 30 minutes. Leave to cool, then strain through a fine sieve. Refrigerate.

Food Fact

Some quick Italian pasta or vegetable bakes (see p38) make great use of mozzarella – it makes a good, cheap and nutritious topping. Buffalo mozzarella is considered the king of mozzarellas. It uses buffalo milk, which results in the cheese tasting extremely mild and creamy. A good mozzarella should come in liquid to keep it moist and should tear easily into chunks.

Food Fact

A classic simple supper is a traditional Shepherd's Pie. It can be made from cold, left-over roast lamb, but you can also make it from fresh minced lamb. If you use beef, it becomes a cottage pie.

Tasty Tip

A good mayonnaise makes a really great accompaniment to chunky chips (see p14), and for speed it can be made in a food processor: blend the mustard, yolk, seasoning and lemon juice briefly, then, with the motor running, slowly pour in the oil. When you are making the mayonnaise, you need to ensure that the ingredients are all at room temperature, or they may curdle.

Food Fact

Spanish tapas is the original fast food, and tortilla, or Spanish omelette, makes a fantastic quick supper. Regarded by some as the national dish of Spain, this substantial omelette is traditionally made from eggs, potatoes and onions, though it is also a good way of using up any left-over ingredients, such as a few cold potatoes, some left-over peas or a slice of bacon that might otherwise go to waste. The choice of potatoes, whether freshly cooked or left over, is important. Use even-sized waxy potatoes, which will not break up during cooking – Maris Bard, Charlotte or Pentland Javelin are all good choices.

Tasty Tip

A quick horseradish sauce makes a great accompaniment to a steak (see p28) – the two can normally be put together in just a few minutes. As your steak cooks, mix together 2 tablespoons of grated horseradish (from a jar) with 3 tablespoons each of Greek yogurt and low-calorie mayonnaise. Add 3 finely chopped spring onions, a squeeze of lime and salt and pepper to taste. And that's it!

Helpful Hint

One of the joys of making simple suppers is that you can find the time to try lots of different types and styles of food. To make the most of this, it is a good idea to avoid bulk buying and, instead, to buy small amounts of fresh food. This means that you will have more flexibility about what you cook and you will not have to plan menus in advance. More importantly, your meals will be more tasty and nutritious – some foods can lose their flavour and nutritional value quite soon after purchase.

First published in 2012 by
FLAME TREE PUBLISHING LTD
Crabtree Hall, Crabtree Lane, Fulham,
London, SW6 6TY, United Kingdom
www.flametreepublishing.com

permission of the copyright holder • The CIP record for this book is available from the British Library • Printed in China

NOTE: Recipes using uncooked eggs should be avoided by infants, the elderly, pregnant women and anyone suffering from an illness.

18 17 16 15 14 13 12   10 9 8 7 6 5 4 3 2 1

ISBN: 978-0-85775-612-1

ACKNOWLEDGEMENTS: Authors: Catherine Atkinson, Juliet Barker, Gina Steer, Vicki Smallwood, Carol Tennant, Mari Mererid Williams, Elizabeth Wolf-Cohen and Simone Wright. Photography: Colin Bowling, Paul Forrester and Stephen Brayne. Home Economists and Stylists: Jacqueline Bellefontaine, Mandy Phipps, Vicki Smallwood and Penny Stephens. All props supplied by Barbara Stewart at Surfaces. Publisher and Creative Director: Nick Wells. Editorial: Catherine Taylor, Sarah Goulding, Marcus Hardie, Gina Steer and Karen Fitzpatrick. Design and Production: Chris Herbert, Mike Spender, Colin Rudderham and Helen Wall.